CW01642025

CONTENTS

DRINKS, DINNER & DEATH

The True Story of Dennis Nilsen

(Book 4 British Criminals)

by Alan R. Warren

Copyrights

Drinks, Dinner & Death

The True Story of Dennis Nilsen

(Book 4 British Criminals)

by Alan R. Warren

Published by
RJ Parker Publishing

March 2019

ISBN 978-1987902617

Printed in Canada

ENTER TO WIN

Monthly KINDLE HD FIRE Giveaway

***

Drawing each month on the 30th...

***

Enter to WIN
(No Purchase Necessary)

Click HERE http://www.rjparkerpublishing.com/Win-a-Kindle.html

Book Synopsis

In the middle-classed neighborhood of Muswell Hill, underneath a spectacular residence located at 23 Cranley Gardens, a gruesome discovery was about to be unearthed. While working on drainage pipes of the house at that location, a plumber discovered several bones and a flesh-like substance covering the inside of the pipes.

The pipes led to the top floor apartment of the residence. It was rented to Dennis Nilsen, a 37-year old, quiet, soft-spoken civil servant. Nilsen was also a retired policeman with military service.

Shockingly, the police were about to discover Dennis Nilsen was also one of Britain's worst serial killers.

Introduction

On February 8, 1983, Michael Cattran was sent out to check the drainpipes at the residence of 23 Cranley Gardens, in the middle-classed neighborhood of Muswell Hill, London. Cattran was an employee of Dyno-Rod, an emergency drainage and plumbing company. February was always the worst time of year to go on these types of calls, since the ground was frozen, the weather was cold, and working outside was brutal.

After arriving at the location that evening, he removed the drain cover on the side of the house. He discovered there was a strange fatty-like substance blocking the drain, with tiny bones mixed in. Cattran thought it was likely somebody had been flushing the bones and uneaten bits of Kentucky Fried Chicken in the toilet. It was getting dark by then and he knew he wouldn't have enough time to clean out the entire drain that night. He would have to return in the morning to finish the job.

The next morning at 7 a.m., Cattran informed

his supervisor what he had found upon initial inspection of the Cranley residence the night before. His supervisor decided to go with him to see what it was they were dealing with. Throughout the day, the two men worked on the drainage system guessing that the bone and flesh-like substance was coming from the apartment on the top floor.

The job was going along as expected until they discovered what looked like a human hand. They called the police immediately. When the police arrived, they took the hand and some of the fleshy substance to the mortuary at Hornsey. The mortuary confirmed that those samples were all of human origin. The police returned to the house and waited for the upstairs tenant to come home.

Dennis Nilsen, who lived in the top floor apartment, returned home from work at precisely 5:15 p.m. He entered the lobby of the building, removed his jacket and shoes upon entering so he wouldn't track any of the snow and mud upstairs to his apartment.

Just then, the two policemen that had been waiting approached him and introduced themselves. They told Nilsen that they were there because of the problems with the apartment building's drainage pipes. He asked, "since when do the police care about drainage or plumbing?" They responded that they needed to see Nilsen's apartment to discuss the matter further.

Nilsen escorted Detective Chief Inspector Jay and another officer to his apartment and let them in. The detective informed Nilsen that the drains had been plugged by human flesh and bone. Nilsen responded that he thought it was awful. The detective, not wanting to waste time, asked him straight out where the body was. Nilsen, without hesitating, told him that it was in the plastic bags in the kitchen.

The policemen opened one of the bags and found several body parts inside. Nilsen was arrested and sent to the police station with two other officers to be interviewed. On the drive to the station, one of the officers asked Nilsen how many bodies there were. They had found 5 or 6 large kitchen bags full of bones and flesh before they left. So they knew there was more than one body. Nilsen responded by saying, “One body, no, 15 or 16.”

CHAPTER 1: EARLY YEARS

Dennis Andrew Nilsen was born on November 23, 1945, in Fraserburgh, Aberdeenshire, the largest shellfish port on the east coast of Scotland. As a result of its' marine influence, and proximity to the sea, the climate is quite mild throughout the year with lots of rain.

Dennis was the middle child of three born to Elizabeth Whyte and Olav Moksheim. Olav Jr. was the oldest child, and Sylvia was the youngest. His parents were originally from Norway, but relocated to Scotland during the Nazi occupation in 1942. The couple moved into her parent's house after they were married. By all accounts, the marriage was a distant one. Olav was always away with the Free Norwegian Forces and made no attempt to spend any time with his family. By 1948, the couple had divorced. Olav left the area and was no longer part of his children's life.

Dennis became close with his grandfather, Andrew Whyte. The two of them would spend most of their time walking the beach and sand dunes together. A fisherman by trade, his grandfather would be gone fishing for long bouts of time. His absence left Dennis feeling quite lonely at home. His siblings were around, however, he never grew to become close with them.

In October 1951, Dennis' grandfather, only 62 years old, suddenly died of a heart attack while fishing in the North Sea. His body was brought back home and taken to his house for a funeral.

When Dennis returned home from school that day, he found his mother crying in their living room. He asked her what was wrong. She asked Dennis if he wanted to see his grandfather. Of course, he said yes. With no warning, Dennis' mother took him to the kitchen, where his grandfather was laying dead in an open coffin.

Dennis had no idea that his grandfather was even sick. The shock of seeing his grandfather like that was something that would stay with him the rest of his life. It would also shape the way he dealt with all his future relationships. From then on, he had a great fear that people in his life would abandon him without notice.

Dennis became withdrawn after his grandfather's death and refused to be involved in any of his family events or activities. He would often be seen sitting alone in the harbor watching the herring boats.

One day, on one of his walks along the beach, he waded out into the ocean until he was submerged beneath the water. He could feel himself being dragged out into the sea. When he realized what was happening, he panicked and screamed. He believed that a great thing then happened-his grandfather came to recue him. A great sense of calm came over him. This event led to Dennis going out into the water more often, submerging himself like before, and waiting for his grandfather to come rescue him.

Shortly after this, his mother moved into her own place with the three children. She married for a second time to a man named Andrew Scott. Dennis didn't like his stepfather. Scott was extremely strict, and disciplined him for even the smallest of things. Whereas, his older brother Olav would never be punished. He seemed to be his stepfather's favorite. Dennis grew to become very jealous of his brother.

In 1955, the family moved to Strichen, about 12 km southwest of where they were living. It was around this time when Dennis started to become close to his baby sister, Sylvia. She was by now old enough to interact with him and the two played games together.

When Dennis was in his teens, he started to find himself attracted to other young men. This confused him, and he was ashamed to tell anybody. He kept his sexuality hidden from all his family and friends because of how badly they spoke of homosexuals.

Also around this time, Dennis began to fondle

and touch his sister sexually. According to Dennis, he did this to see if he could be sexually attracted to a female, and to see if the gay feelings towards young men would go away. Dennis later admitted there was another young man that had touched him sexually around that time, but he didn't like the experience.

Dennis shared a bed with his older brother Olav. On several occasions after Olav fell asleep, Dennis would fondle or touch his brother sexually. Once, Olav woke up and caught Dennis . He confronted him. After that, his brother belittled him publicly and called him a 'hen.' (Scottish for a girl)

When Dennis was 14 years old, he decided to join the Army Cadet Force. He considered this to be an escape from his parents and the stifling small town in which he lived. In school, he excelled in History and Art but wasn't good at sports. When Dennis finished school, he got a job at a cannery. That only lasted three weeks because he wanted to do something different with his life.

In September 1961, Dennis decided to enlist in the army. For the next nine years, he was assigned to the Army Catering Corps at St. Omer Barracks in Aldershot. There, he trained to become a chef. He later described the time he spent in the army as a chef as the best time of his life.

While he was stationed in Aldershot, he would never shower with the other soldiers. He was afraid he would become excited in front of them, and his sexuality would no longer be a secret. Instead, he would wash himself in the bathroom, where he had the privacy to masturbate. Quite often, he found himself sexually attracted to the other soldiers.

In 1964, Nilsen passed the catering exam and was stationed at the first battalion of the Royal Fusiliers in Osnabruck, West Germany, serving as a private. Later, his fellow soldiers described him as very shy and quiet, noticing that he would often get drunk in order to ease his shyness.

Nilsen said that it was during these drunken moments that he would fantasize about having sex with different men. The men he fantasized about were always young, thin, and passive. He never acted on his fantasies though. He figured he would be beaten severely and probably discharged from the service.

His fantasies gradually evolved, or rather devolved, to have very dark undertones. The men he dreamed about having sex with would be unconscious, and sometimes even dead. That way, they wouldn't know Nilsen had sex with them. Nilsen admitted that there were a few instances when he was drinking with other soldiers and pretended to be passed out. He secretly hoped that they would have sex with him while he was unconscious. But to his dismay, it never happened

In 1967, Nilsen was deployed to Aden, South Yemen, as a cook for the Al Mansoura Prison. That assignment was a much more dangerous station than the one in Germany. Often, there were attacks by the locals, and in fact, several of the men he worked with were killed. The attacks usually occurred traveling between the barracks and the prison. On one occasion, Nilsen was attacked and beaten unconscious by a taxi driver. He woke up in the trunk of a car. He was able to escape by hitting the cab driver over the head with a tire iron he found in the trunk.

While stationed in Yemen, Nilsen had his own private bedroom, and his fantasies became even more elaborate. He placed a freestanding mirror on the side of his bed, so he could see only his own body, without his face. When he masturbated, he sometimes pretended he was an unconscious man being sexually dominated. Alternatively, Nilsen sometimes fantasized he was the dominant one, and the body he was watching was that of an unconscious or dead man.

Nilsen also fantasized about having sex with the soldiers he had seen killed. He imagined they were naked and spread-eagled on his bed while having sex. And now, he added washing the corpse to the fantasy before having sex with them.

In 1968, Nilsen was transferred to the Seaton Barracks in Plymouth. He was assigned to serve with the Argyll and Sutherland Highlanders, where he cooked for approximately 30 soldiers daily. In 1969, he was assigned to Cyprus, and then to Berlin, Germany. While Nilsen was in Berlin, he hired a female prostitute to have intercourse with him. He thought this would give him bragging rights around the other soldiers. He later described this encounter as depressing and overrated.

In 1971, Nilsen was assigned to cook for the Queen's Royal Guard. He was promoted to the rank of corporal. He kept this position until October 1972, when he resigned from the military. After his resignation, he moved home with his family in Strichen, and remained there for the next three months in order to figure out what his next career move would be.

During this time with his family, they watched a documentary on television about homosexuals. His family was openly disgusted by what they learned. Despite knowing how they felt, Dennis told his mother he was a homosexual. The family argument that ensued ended in Nilsen leaving and never speaking to any of his family again, with the exception of a few sporadic letters exchanged with his mother.

Nilsen decided to move to London and join the Metropolitan Police. In April 1973, he completed his training and was posted to Willesden Green. As a junior constable, he made several arrests for minor infractions, but nothing major where he had to subdue anybody.

During the summer of 1973, Nilsen started to frequent gay pubs, and have actual encounters with men he met there. He later claimed he was looking for a long-term relationship and not just one-night stands. He thought those types of relationships would destroy his soul. He was also conflicted between his lifestyle as a gay man and being a policeman. At the time, the two were really at odds. So, in December that year, he resigned from the police force.

A few months earlier his stepfather passed away, leaving Nilsen £1,000. This gave him the freedom to not have to find work immediately. Later, he got a job as a security guard, but it was part-time and intermittent.

In May 1974, Nilsen found a full-time job as a civil servant at the job center on Denmark Street. He was assigned the task of finding work for unskilled laborers. There, he was considered to be quiet and very respectable by his work colleagues. In 1979, he became Acting Executive Officer, a job that came with additional supervisory responsibilities. Nilsen excelled in his new position, and in June of 1982, it became his permanent position. With this change came a relocation to Kentish Town, London.

CHAPTER 2: 195 MELROSE AVENUE - VICTIMS

On a cold November day in 1975, Nilsen came out of a London gay pub and saw 20-year-old, David Gallichan, being harassed and threatened by two older men. Nilsen broke up the fight, and walked David back to his room at a hostel in the Cricklewood District.

Nilsen ended up staying the night with David, but according to him, the two of them did not have sex. Instead, they stayed up all night just talking and drinking. The next morning, the two decided they would make great roommates. They just needed to find a larger place to move into.

Out of the remainder of his inheritance from his stepfather, Nilsen found and paid for a ground floor flat in the same area of town, 195 Melrose Avenue. The flat afforded exclusive access to a large garden located at the rear of the property. They both loved this idea since they shared the image of creating a home.

Nilsen was the only one of the two working, so he was deemed the breadwinner, or head of the household. David decorated the home and maintained the garden. From his years in the military, Nilsen was used to giving orders and controlling everything around him. David, on the other hand, was rather passive and took the submissive role, happy to be with Nilsen.

After a year and a half together, the stress of this arrangement started to take a toll on their relationship. David was angry at Nilsen's ordering him around but kept his anger inside. The stress affected their love life, and soon they ended up in separate bedrooms. Eventually, they both brought home other men for one-night stands, adding jealousy to an already stressful situation.

One day in May 1977, Nilsen returned home at 5:15 p.m. to find David gone. He had packed some of his clothes and left, leaving a note explaining he just couldn't continue in the relationship anymore. Nilsen was devastated. The pain of David's leaving brought back unresolved feelings from when he saw his grandfather dead in a coffin.

Later though, Nilsen told a different story of David's leaving. He claimed that after the two had a fight, Nilsen ended the relationship and asked David to leave. Over the next two years, Nilsen brought home several other men, but nothing long-term came out of these encounters. The longest relationship he had after David lasted only a few weeks.

One of these relationships was with Martyn

Hunter-Craig, (real name was Martyn Tucker), an 18-year-old who recently moved to London from Exeter. Craig was diagnosed with emotional problems and attended a special school, where they often questioned his sexuality.

In the book by author Russ Coffey, *'Dennis Nilsen: Conversations with Britain's Most Evil Serial Killer,'* Craig told him:

"I wasn't camp or outrageous as a teenager. I was quite withdrawn, I didn't like it, I didn't want to be that way. I was made to feel quite dirty about it. I've had that hang up ever since, I think I feel wretched and dirty about it. I don't like it but that's the way it is, I can do nothing about it, can I?"

Craig was living in London a few months before meeting Nilsen. To survive, he received a check from Social Security for his disability, did odd jobs here and there, and slept with men for money. On Easter weekend,, Craig approached Nilsen while at an arcade. The two had a nice conversation. They went back to Nilsen's apartment, drank, ate, and had sex. Their dates became a regular monthly event lasting a couple of nights at a time. Craig claimed Nilsen told him from the very first night they were together if he needed somewhere to stay, he was welcome to go to his place.

Later, the media and public were split on whether they could believe Craig's story. There were some that thought a well-dressed, professional man like Nilsen would never invite a social misfit and prostitute back to stay in his apartment.

Craig told the press that Nilsen wanted companionship, and not a sexual relationship, from him. He also claimed that Nilsen even invited him to move into his apartment. Nilsen nicknamed Craig, 'Skip', slang for a man that hung around the docks.

Craig also talked about how Nilsen would sometimes come home from work and explode in a sudden rage. Nilsen thought people were talking about him behind his back, whispering, and making fun of him. Craig mentioned how Nilsen was very strict about his personal hygiene, yet his apartment smelled musty, and he didn't seem to care about how dirty it was. Craig further commented that there seemed to be a smell that followed Nilsen around. Craig eventually stopped going over to Nilsen's apartment sometime later that year.

After Craig, Nilsen completely focused on his work. He stopped going out to bars and picking up men. He said it was harder on him to make an effort to meet someone, invest time trying to get to know the person, only to have him end up leaving. The whole thing made him feel insecure and not good enough for anybody else.

NILSEN, EARLY YEARS

Stephen Dean Holmes

During the Christmas holiday of 1978, Nilsen was alone. Restless, and in need of some company, he went out to a local pub, Cricklewood Arms Pub. While sitting in the pub, looking around for somebody to chat with, he noticed the bartender yelling at a young man, but couldn't hear what all the fuss was about. He heard the young man tell the bartender to "Fuck Off," and storm out the front door. Intrigued, Nilsen got up and chased after the young man to find out what happened.

Turns out, the young man was 14-year-old, Stephen Holmes. He had tried to buy alcohol at the bar but was refused. Nilsen, figuring the man was about 17 years old, invited him over to his place for drinks. Holmes accepted. The two went back to Nilsen's house and drank heavily before falling asleep.

The next morning Nilsen awoke to find

Holmes asleep in his bed. Nilsen slowly and very lightly caressed Holmes while he was still sleeping, not wanting to wake him. While he was doing this, Nilsen started to have a fantasy about Holmes staying with him for the New Years holiday - whether Holmes wanted to or not.

Nilsen walked over to his bedroom dresser, retrieved one of his ties, and got back into bed. He started to caress Holmes again, only this time Holmes began to awaken. Nilsen wrapped the tie around Holmes' neck and strangled him until he was unconscious. Sitting on top of Holmes' stomach, Nilsen masturbated over his body, finishing on his chest.

Nilsen walked into his bathroom and started filling the bathtub with warm water. He dragged Holmes into the bathroom, and placed him face down in the water. He held his head under the water for at least five minutes to make sure that Holmes was dead. He pulled the body out of the tub, laid him on the floor and bound him with ropes. Nilsen wrapped Holmes' body in a curtain and then went back to sleep.

Nilsen planned to store Holmes' body under the floorboards. However, the next day when he awoke, rigor mortis had already set in, making the body too stiff to carry out this plan. He started to panic but then remembered that the body would loosen up if he waited another day or two.

The next day, Nilsen pulled up some of the loose floorboards from his living room. He placed Holmes' body in the space until he could figure out how he would dispose of him. The floorboards were put back in place and Nilsen went on with his day. Holmes' body would remain in that spot for about eight months, until August 11 that year, when Nilsen decided he would have a bonfire and burn the remains.

According to Nilsen's memoir, *"History of a Drowning Boy,"* both of them drank until they passed out. He claimed it wasn't until he woke the next morning that he realized the boy was dead. Nilsen also claimed that the boy had a tie wrapped around his neck, and he was in total shock at all this.

In Brian Master's account, *"Killing for Company,"* Nilsen says he snuggled up to the boy, putting his arm around him, and when he fell asleep, he pulled the blanket off. The boy was on his side facing the other direction. Nilsen caressed his body and became extremely aroused. The thought of morning coming and the boy leaving him filled his mind, causing his heart to pound heavily and sweat to form on his face. When he turned, he saw his tie lying on the floor beside the bed. Nilsen then decided the boy was staying over New Years, even if he didn't want to. So he slowly bent down, grabbed his tie, slipped it around the boy's neck, and strangled him to death.

Andrew Ho

Almost 10 months later, on October 11, 1979, Nilsen picked up Andrew Ho, a foreign student from Hong Kong, at St. Martin's Lane Pub. The two went back to Nilsen's flat for more drinks. Nilsen claimed that Ho started a conversation about bondage and wanted to be paid for it.

Nilsen told Ho to sit still while he bound his feet together. He went to his closet, grabbed a tie, and started to strangle Ho. Quickly realizing the danger, Ho started to scream and struggle. He eventually broke loose, grabbed his clothes, and ran out of the apartment.

Ho went straight to the police station to file a complaint. Shortly after, the police arrived at Nilsen's apartment to question him about the incident. He knew that he had to convince the police that it was simply a mistake, a wild sexual encounter gone awry, and nothing more. Ho didn't want to file an official written report since it would be on record that Ho went home with a strange man, something his family would not understand. So, no charges were filed, and the police closed the case.

Kenneth Ockendon

A mere two months later, on December 3, 1979, Nilsen met a 23-year-old Canadian tourist, Kenneth Ockendon, at a West End (Theatre area of London) pub. Nilsen and Ockendon stayed at the pub for hours talking and drinking. Nilsen found out Ockendon was in town visiting some of his relatives; he offered to show him some of the great landmarks, and Ockendon accepted. Ockendon planned to go home to Canada for the Christmas holiday.

While at the pub, he called his Uncle Gordon, who lived in London, to tell him he needed to come by his place to pick up some money for his trip home. During this phone call, his Uncle could hear music in the background, and Ockendon told his uncle that he was at a jazz pub.

On the way to Nilsen's flat, where they planned on having dinner, the two decided to stop at an off sales place to buy vodka, rum and beer. At the flat, they ate, drank, and made plans about which landmarks to visit. Nilsen told Ockendon that he needed to shower first before they left and went into the bathroom.

Ockendon decided to listen to music while he waited and put on his headphones. Meanwhile, Nilsen quietly sneaked out of the bathroom and slowly crept up behind Ockendon, lifting the headphone cord with both hands as he crept. The cord was long enough that it neither pulled out of the stereo when moved, nor noticed by Ockendon when it was lifted. Nilsen slowly roped the cord around Ockendon's neck and pulled as hard as he could.

Surprised, Ockendon tried to stand using both hands to pull on the cord that was firmly around his neck. However, Nilsen was pulling with such force that Ockendon fell backwards over the sofa and onto the floor. Nilsen dragged Ockendon on his back across the floor until he stopped struggling.

Nilsen stripped Ockendon's body of all his clothes and laid him on the bed. He then took off his own clothes, got into bed, curled up with the corpse, and fell asleep. The next morning, Nilsen took out his Polaroid camera and took several pictures of Ockendon in different poses. He lay with the corpse for several more hours while he watched television. Later that evening, Nilsen wrapped Ockendon's body in plastic garbage bags, and placed him under the same floorboards that also hid the body of Holmes.

While Holmes' body remained under the floorboards, Nilsen would often remove Ockendon's body from under the floorboards. He sat him in an armchair, and talked to the body while watching television and drinking. Some nights he would bring the body into bed with him, sleep with it all night, and put it back under the floor in the morning before leaving for work.

When Ockendon didn't show up at his Uncle's house the next day to pick up the money for his trip, his uncle called the police. After checking with Ockendon's hotel, the police discovered that his bill was paid and all his possessions were still in his room. Ockendon's parents were called and they flew to London. They made several appeals on television and in newspapers for information about their missing son.

In February 1983, Nilsen gave police more information about his encounter with Ockendon. He told them that the two met in a pub that was popular among gay men. Nilsen commented on Ockendon's camera, and the two ended up talking for hours. Nilsen claimed he took Ockendon on a tour of London's landmarks, such as Trafalgar Square and the House of Parliament.

Nilsen also claimed the two went back to his flat, where they ate and listened to music. The pair ran out to get some rum and beer at an off sales place. They returned to Nilsen's flat and continued to drink and listen to music.

It was about 1 a.m. when Nilsen tightened the headphone cord around Ockendon's neck and shouted, "Let me listen to the music as well." Ockendon didn't struggle at all, and after he was dead, Nilsen poured another drink of rum for himself.

Nilsen stripped and washed Ockendon's body in his bathtub before placing him on his bed. He drank some more, and listened to more of the records before crawling into bed with the corpse. He then had sex with it.

Ockendon was now a prop in his fantasy. As such, he had to remove any reminder of who the person had been. So, he wrapped all Ockendon's possessions in bags, and put them in the garbage bin. Then he placed the body in his kitchen cupboard.

Nilsen ran to the store to buy a Polaroid camera. When he returned to the apartment, he removed the body from the cupboard, and laid it on the bed. He took at least 15 pictures of himself naked with Ockendon's body in different positions, to keep a record of his acts.

Martyn Duffey

On May 17, 1980, Nilsen was on his way home from work when he exited the train at the Euston railway station. He came across a young man who looked like he had been sleeping there. It was 16-year-old Martyn Duffey. He ran away from his home in Liverpool about a week earlier. He was not only homeless, but had not eaten much all that week since leaving.

Nilsen told him that he had a spare room and could feed him dinner if he wanted to come to his flat. Duffey gladly accepted, and the pair went to Nilsen's house. They had dinner and drinks, and soon Duffey fell asleep on Nilsen's bed.

Like before, Nilsen placed a tie around Duffey's neck. Sitting on his chest, Nilsen pulled the tie tightly. He held his grip while the boy struggled. When Duffey fell unconscious, Nilsen dragged him into his kitchen, drowned him in his sink, and took him into the bath where he washed his body.

Nilsen kept Duffey's body for two days. He either sat him upright in the armchair conversing with the dead body, or laid him on his bed where he would kiss, fondle and masturbate on the stomach of the corpse. Before he left for work each day, he would place the body in a cupboard. After a couple of days, the body became bloated, so he stored it under the floorboards with the others.

When the police interviewed Nilsen, he told them that he remembered meeting Duffey on the day he returned home from a union conference in Southport. He added that he always liked those types of trips, since they gave him an opportunity to look for young runaways that hung around the train stations.

Nilsen said he couldn't remember much about their conversations or activities back at his apartment because Duffey was extremely tired and quiet. It was only about two hours before Duffey needed to go to bed. Yet in the book *"Killing for Company,"* Nilsen remembered sitting astride of Duffey, remembered his arms trapped in the comforter, and remembered strangling Duffey with great force in the pitch-black room. Nilsen even remembered feeling the wetness of Duffey's urine on his bottom while sitting on top of Duffey.

He also remembered Duffey was still alive after the strangulation. So Nilsen dragged his body to the kitchen and drowned him in the sink. He then moved the body to the bathroom, where they both bathed together. Then he remembered carrying the body back to his bed.

According to Nilsen's memoir *"History of a Drowning Boy,"* he thought that Duffey was the youngest-looking body he had ever seen, which was a real turn-on for him. Nilsen claimed that Duffey had a set of cooking knives with him. In order to avoid attracting any attention, Nilsen let the knives rust before throwing them away. After killing Duffey, Nilsen went back to the Euston train station, retrieved Duffey's checked suitcase, and disposed of it.

Nilsen was really taken with Duffey's body. He continued to use it in his fantasies for much longer than he had the others. Not only would he sleep and have sex with the corpse, but he would also remove the body from under the floorboards, sit it in an armchair, and talk to it for hours.

In the last six months of 1980, Nilsen killed five more victims, and attempted to murder one other. Only one of those killed was later identified as 26-year-old William David Sutherland. Nilsen claimed to have only vague recollections of the unidentified victims, but he could recall how he murdered each one.

William Sutherland

In August of 1980, Nilsen met Billy Sutherland in a gay pub in Soho. William Sutherland was a 26-year-old father of one from Edinburgh, working as a rent boy (male prostitute). Sutherland had grown up in the slums of North Edinburgh. He moved in with his girlfriend Donna and they had a daughter together. In order to support his family, Sutherland moved to London to find work. Donna joined him there for short periods of time throughout the year.

Nilsen picked up Sutherland by offering him money to come back to his place and have sex with him. Nilsen couldn't remember many of the details of that night, other than it was like the previous victims...he strangled Sutherland with a tie, bathed him in water, and had sex with the body on his bed.

Sutherland's girlfriend, Donna, stopped receiving phone calls from Sutherland and became worried. It was out of character for him not to call and talk to their daughter. However, the mystery of his disappearance wasn't solved until 1983, after Nilsen was caught, and his crimes were revealed in the newspapers. Donna suspected Nilsen was the reason Sutherland went missing years before. She called Billy's father, who contacted the police. The police later showed Sutherland's picture to Nilsen, and he confirmed that he had killed the man.

Over the next year, Nilsen murdered between five and eight others, and attempted to murder at least one more, Douglas Stewart. Nilsen claimed to have a poor memory of this time period.

UNIDENTIFIED MURDER VICTIM #5

Despite being unable to remember much about his next victim, Nilsen admitted that in September 1980, he met an Irish man with rough work hands at the Cricklewood Arms pub. He guessed the man to be about 27 to 30 years old. Nilsen later claimed he made this victim up, and that he never existed.

UNIDENTIFIED MURDER VICTIM #6

A month later in October, Nilsen met another victim at the Salisbury Arms Pub. He identified the man as a Filipino or Mexican prostitute, between the ages of 20 and 30, 5-foot 10-inches tall, slender, with gypsy-like features. He lured the man back to his place with an offer of money and drinks. Nilsen didn't remember any of the details of the murder.

UNIDENTIFIED MURDER VICTIM #7

In November 1980, Nilsen was walking along Charing Cross Road when he encountered a man that was sleeping in the doorway of a vacant business. The man was around 20-years-old, emaciated, pale complexion, with several missing teeth. Nilsen hailed a cab and took the man home with him after offering to feed him dinner, and give him a warm bed to sleep in.

Nilsen commented that while he was strangling this victim, the man moved his legs in a cycling motion as if he was riding a bicycle. Nilsen believed the man had a very hard life, and killing him was like taking candy from a baby.

UNIDENTIFIED MURDER VICTIM #8

Nilsen couldn't remember if the next victim was killed in late November or early December. He described the man as a hippy, between the ages of 25 and 30. He said they met on the road one night, in the West End, after all the pubs had closed. But Nilsen claimed later this was another fabricated victim, and it never happened.

By this time, the bodies Nilsen had stowed under the floorboards began to smell and attract insects, especially during the summer. When he removed the floorboards and saw that quite a few of the corpses had maggots crawling out of the eye sockets and mouths, he placed deodorants in the area and sprayed insecticides about twice a day. Regardless, the odor became unbearable.

Nilsen decided that it was time to start having bonfires again, like he did with his live-in boyfriend years before. Only this time, he would make them communal and invite all the neighbors. Nilsen dissected each of the bodies that he had killed since 1979, and burned them in these bonfires. Nobody suspected the smell emanating from the bonfire was burning flesh. The bonfire had been built on top of a waste ground, and Nilsen placed old tires on the fire as an excuse for the odor.

UNIDENTIFIED MURDER VICTIM #9

On January 4, 1981, Nilsen met his next victim at the Golden Lion Pub in Soho. He described the man as an 18-year-old, blue-eyed, Scot, who was wearing a green tracksuit with trainers. The two men went back to Nilsen's Melrose Avenue apartment for a drinking contest. The man passed out. Nilsen said he couldn't remember the murder, or how he disposed of the body.

UNIDENTIFIED MURDER VICTIM #10

In February 1981, Nilsen met another unknown victim in the West End after the pubs had closed. Again, he offered the man drinks and sex if he came home with him. He described the man to be in his early twenties, about 5-foot 9-inches tall, very slim, and from Belfast. Like a lot of the other victims, Nilsen said he couldn't remember much about the murder or disposal of the body.

UNIDENTIFIED MURDER VICTIM #11

At a food stall in Leicester Square, in April of 1981, Nilsen met his next victim. He described the man to be a skinhead, about 20-years old. He lured the man back to his place with the promise of free alcohol and a meal. Nilsen described a tattoo that the man had on his neck. It said, 'cut here.' The man talked about how tough he was, and how many times he beat people up.

After Nilsen strangled this victim, he hung the naked body from the ceiling in his bedroom for 24 hours before placing it under the floorboards. Like two of the previously listed victims, Nilsen later recanted his confession, saying that he fabricated this victim as well.

Malcolm Barlow

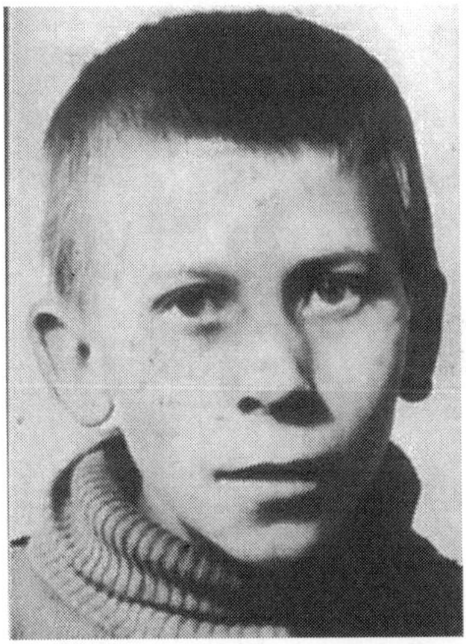

Nilsen's final victim was Malcolm Barlow, a 23-year-old man whom Nilsen found slumped up against a wall on September 17, 1981. Nilsen discovered Barlow had taken epilepsy medication, which caused his legs to be too weak to walk. Nilsen carried Barlow back to his place, so he could get warm. After a couple of hours, Barlow didn't seem to be getting any better. Nilsen walked to a local phone box, since his phone had been disconnected, and called an ambulance for Barlow.

Born in Rotherham, near Sheffield, Barlow suffered from epilepsy from a very early age. His mother died when he was 11, and he was sent to live with his aunt Doreen. However, she found him to be unmanageable. Barlow was caught stealing, lying, and even sleeping with men in order to blackmail them. Eventually, she kicked him out of her home, and he ended up living in hostels and on welfare.

After being released from the hospital the next day, Barlow returned to Nilsen's house to thank him for helping him. But Nilsen wasn't home. Barlow had nowhere to go, so he waited on the front stairs of the apartment building for Nilsen to come home. When Nilsen returned and saw Barlow waiting there, he was bothered; but invited him in anyway.

The two men ate dinner, drank rum, and soon Barlow was unconscious on the sofa. Nilsen worried that he might have to call another ambulance for Barlow. He was also worried that the police might get involved. This made him very annoyed.

After twenty minutes with Barlow still unconscious, Nilsen strangled him. He kept Barlow's body in bed with him that night. The next morning, he stuffed Barlow's body in his kitchen closet, and went to work. Nilsen didn't mention this killing in his memoir, claiming he didn't remember much about it.

In October 1981, Nilsen's landlord decided to renovate and sell the house on Melrose Avenue. He offered Nilsen £1,000 to vacate the property. Nilsen accepted the offer and found a new residence at 23D Cranley Gardens in the Muswell Hill area in Northern London. On the last day he lived on Melrose Avenue, he had a bonfire to burn his final five victims. After the fire, he checked the ashes thoroughly with a rake to make sure there was nothing recognizable.

195 MELROSE AVENUE

POLICE SEARCHING DENNIS NILSEN'S GARDEN FOR REMAINS

CHAPTER 3: 23D CRANLEY GARDENS

Nilsen's new place was quite different than the one he had at Melrose Avenue. It was a large home that had been renovated into several apartments, and he rented the apartment in the attic of the house. Being in an attic caused him quite a dilemma. This new place left him without a garden to burn any bodies in, and no floorboards to stow bodies under.

Paul Nobbs

In November 1981, about a month after he moved into his new apartment, Nilsen picked up a 19-year-old student named Paul Nobbs. Nobbs was majoring in Slavic studies at London University. The two men met at the Golden Lion Pub in Soho. The night they met, Nobbs was having an argument at the bar with another man. Nilsen approached the men and calmed the situation. Nobbs thought Nilsen was a kind man for diffusing the encounter, and the two men sat together at a table and drank.

Nilsen invited Nobbs back to his flat for more drinks and to watch the movie 'Panorama.' After they returned to his apartment, they drank heavily. Nobbs decided to stay the night, but he needed to call his mother to let her know. He called his mother on a phone box and told her that he wouldn't be back that night.

The two men went to bed and Nobbs tried to initiate sexual intercourse with Nilsen. Nilsen told him that he didn't do penetration; so the two just went to sleep. In the middle of the night, Nobbs awakened with a terrible pain in his neck. He got up quickly, ran into the bathroom, and looked in the mirror to see what was causing the pain.

Nobbs noticed that his eyes were bloodshot. He was also very dizzy and disorientated, but had no idea what was wrong. He returned to bed, lay down, and fell asleep. At 6 a.m., he woke again with a similar pain in his neck. Again, he went into the bathroom to look. This time he saw bruising around his neck.

When he returned to the bedroom, Nilsen was sitting up and asking what was the matter. Nobbs just shrugged his shoulders indicating he didn't know. Nilsen suggested that he go see a doctor, but Nobbs went back to bed and fell asleep.

This time, Nilsen started to strangle him. Nobbs quickly woke up, broke away, and ran out of the apartment, screaming. Since Nobbs was creating a huge commotion, Nilsen didn't go after him. He remained quiet in his apartment.

Nobbs went to the hospital where the doctors told him someone had attacked him, and attempted to strangle him. Nobbs was too embarrassed to go to the police and make a report.

John Howlett

It was three months before Nilsen got the courage to try and lure another man home to kill. In January of 1982, Nilsen met John Howlett, a 23-year-old man from High Wycombe, at a pub in Leicester Square. Howlett was 5-foot 10-inches tall, with a very toned body. Howlett left home while he was still a teenager. He found a job with a carnival, traveled the country, and worked at different fairs. At the pub, the two men drank most of the night. But when Nilsen invited Howlett back to his place, he said he had to go because he had an early morning.

A month later, in March, the two met up again in the same pub. This time it was Howlett that approached Nilsen. He remembered him from his last visit in January. The two men talked and drank together before Nilsen invited Howlett back to his apartment for dinner.

The pair left the pub and went back to Nilsen's apartment. There, Nilsen cooked dinner while they had more drinks. They decided to watch a movie. During the movie, Howlett asked Nilsen if it was okay to lie on his bed to get some rest. Nilsen told him that it was okay. But really, Nilsen was annoyed.

When the movie ended, Nilsen went into the bedroom and found that Howlett had taken off his cloths and got in bed. Nilsen sarcastically said,

"I didn't know you were moving in? Perhaps you should call a cab." Howlett moaned and said nothing. Nilsen didn't like Howlett. He didn't find him attractive. So he went back to the living room to have another drink and think about what he was going to do.

Sometime over the next hour, the two men struggled, both trying to strangle the other. Nilsen eventually won the battle however, and Howlett fell unconscious. Nilsen was using an upholstery strap to strangle Howlett, but after three attempts, he continued to regain consciousness. Nilsen finally dragged the unconscious Howlett into the bathroom and drowned him in the tub. The struggle left scratches and bruises all over Nilsen's body, and some were around his neck in clear view.

Nilsen didn't mention this murder in his memoir. We only have the confession he made to the police years later:

"Summoning up all of my strength, I forced him back down and his head struck the rim of the head-rest on the bed. He still struggled fiercely so that now he was half off the bed. In about a minute, he had gone limp. There was blood on the bed, I assumed it was from his head. I checked and he was still breathing deep, rasping breaths. I tightened my grip on him again around his neck for another minute or so. I let go my grip again, and he appeared to be dead."

"I stood up, the dog was barking in the next room, so I

went to pacify it. I was shaking all over with the stress of the struggle. I really thought he was going to get the better of me. I returned and was shocked to see that he had started breathing again. I looped the material around his neck again, pulled it as tight as I could and held on for what must have been two or three minutes. when I released my grip, he had stopped breathing."

Nilsen decided to dispose of Howlett's body piece by piece. He covered his bathroom floor with plastic garbage bags, dragged the body out from his closet, and dissected it there. He cut off the soft parts of the body and flushed them down the toilet.

The process was taking hours. So, Nilsen thought it might be quicker to boil the flesh down to a soup-like mixture. It would also make it a lot easier to flush down the toilet, avoiding any backups or overflows. When the head was cooked enough, he scooped out the brains and flushed them as well.

The larger bones and parts that were firm were wrapped up in plastic bags. He laid those out on the floor, packed them with salt, and left them for the garbage man to pick up. Nilsen kept a few of the larger pieces; he thought the garbage man might not take all of them, and questions might arise.

Carl Stottor

CARL STOTTOR TODAY

In May of 1982, Nilsen went to the Black Cap Pub in Camden, where he met a 21-year-old man named Carl Stottor. Nilsen noticed Stottor sitting alone at the bar. He looked sad, so Nilsen approached him and offered to buy him another beer. Stottor accepted, and Nilsen sat beside him. The two started up a conversation.

Stottor later commented that Nilsen was the kind of person you knew all your life, even if you had just met him. Stottor felt at ease with Nilsen. Safe enough that he told him about a previous abusive relationship, where his boyfriend would call him all sorts of names and often physically beat him. Stottor was too scared of the ex-boyfriend to go to the police and file a report against him.

Stottor also commented that not only was Nilsen very kind and comforting, he in fact reminded him of his first boyfriend. He felt a real connection between with Nilsen. That night, they drank heavily before going to Nilsen's apartment, where they drank even more. Stottor fell asleep on a sleeping bag on the floor.

The next thing Stottor remembered was waking up with Nilsen sitting on top of him saying 'stay still'. He thought Nilsen was trying to help him out of the sleeping bag since his shirt was caught up in the zipper. Instead, Nilsen wrapped his hands around Stottor's neck and began to choke him until he was unconscious.

Stottor remembered waking up again to the sound of water running in the bathtub. Nilsen came into the room and dragged him into the bathroom, putting him in the tub facedown in the water. Nilsen held Stottor's head under the water, pulling him up every few minutes to see if he was still alive. After several attempts, Nilsen quit. He must have thought Stottor was dead.

Stottor was only unconscious when Nilsen pulled him out of the bathtub and placed him sitting upright in an armchair. Sometime during the night, Nilsen realized that Stottor was still alive. He placed him on the bed, gave him a heart massage, and covered him with blankets. Over the next two days, Stottor said he would lapse in and out of consciousness.

When Stottor regained his strength and was fully awake, he questioned Nilsen about what had happened. Nilsen told Stottor that he was having a nightmare in the sleeping bag. He was screaming, so Nilsen went to wake him, only to find him stuck in the zipper of the sleeping bag. Nilsen continued to say that Stottor was in such a panic, that he must have been in shock. So he placed him in a tub full of cold water to revive him.

Stottor cleaned himself up as much as he could. Nilsen walked him to the nearby train station telling him to stay in touch and hopefully they could get together again soon.

Carl Stottor told what happened during his time with Nilsen:

"When he attacked me, I was jolted awake to find the zipper wrapped tightly around my neck. I presumed I'd become tangled in my sleep (Stottor was sleeping in a sleeping bag) but Nilsen was behind me, kneeing me in the back and telling me to keep still. At first, I thought he was trying to free me, but of course I was being strangled."

Stottor continued, *"The pain was incredible. No air going into my lungs and all I could feel was the teeth of the zipper digging into my neck as he pulled it tighter. I briefly felt blood from the wound trickling over my skin, then I passed out."*

Stottor claimed he was tortured for two days before Nilsen let him go.

Stottor got off the train and went directly to the hospital, where he was treated for burst blood vessels in his face, water in his lungs, and several cuts on his neck. It was about two weeks before Stottor went to the police. *"Back then the police would just sweep the gay thing under the carpets,"* claimed Stottor.

In the summer of 2009, the mayor of London at the time, Boris Johnson, announced plans to open a museum that would include artifacts from Nilsen's murder spree. Stottor said he felt the mayor was being distasteful and insensitive.

Graham Allen

In September of 1982, Nilsen was leaving work when he saw a man, 28-year-old Graham Allen, trying to hail a cab in Piccadilly. He showed obvious signs of being a drug addict so no cab would stop and pick him up. Nilsen offered him a ride in his cab and Allen accepted.

On the ride, Nilsen learned that Allen was from Glasgow, had a girlfriend named Lesley, and a son named Shane. Allen was a tall, rugged, heterosexual who went by the nickname of 'Pugsy.' He was aggressive and uncultured. Allen was supporting himself with casual jobs in civil service but wanted to pursue a career in writing. He had a blog website which was still online at the time of this writing: http://memoiresofaheroinhead.blogspot.com/

Allen had a bad addiction to heroin. He stole from businesses or people in order to get the money to pay for it. His girlfriend, Lesley, figured he went to find heroin the night he went missing. And maybe he was going to mug a gay man for the money.

Sometime during the cab ride, Nilsen talked Allen into coming back to his apartment for dinner. In all likelihood, it was an easy thing for him to do since Allen was intent on mugging him anyway.

When they got back to the apartment, Nilsen offered to make them each an omelet. Allen was sitting at the kitchen table with his back to the kitchen. After he was about three quarters the way through his omelet, he passed out, still sitting upright in the chair.

According to what he told police in his confession years later, Nilsen sat down at the table with a drink, and just watched Allen for a while. He then approached Allen, unable to tell if he was still breathing or not. Allen had egg hanging out of his mouth. Nilsen gathered the dirty dishes from the table and took them into the kitchen.

Nilsen returned with his work tie wrapped tightly around both hands and strangled Allen. Nilsen claimed he couldn't remember what he used on him, but he was dead. He even suggested to the detectives maybe the omelet killed him. But when they brought up the issue of the red marks on Allen's neck, he responded by saying it must have been him then.

After Nilsen strangled Allen to death, he placed his body on his bed. He kept the body there for three days, caressing, kissing, and masturbating each night. He placed the body in the armchair before he left for work. When he returned from work, he told the corpse all about his day.

After a few days, the body started to smell badly. It was also becoming too stiff to work with, so Nilsen dissected the corpse on his kitchen floor. Like before, he boiled and cooked the flesh of different parts of the body, and placed some of the remains in plastic kitchen bags. Some he would flush down the toilet, and some he let drain out with the water from the tub.

Allen was at first considered another 'unknown victim' until the police were able to identify him from the metal plate in his jaw.

Surprisingly, there were two men who visited Nilsen's apartment after the murder of Allen that survived. The first was 20-year-old Trevor Simpson. Simpson met Nilsen on Wednesday, December 22, at a Soho pub. Simpson had just been released from prison after serving a six-month sentence for car hijacking in Belgium.

After the two men met, talked, and had a couple of drinks, Nilsen invited him back to his apartment. Simpson was a heterosexual, so when it got late, Nilsen offered him a place to sleep in one of his armchairs, while Nilsen slept in the bed.

Simpson, newly out of prison, had no place to stay. The next morning, Nilsen told him that he could crash there until he found something. Simpson accepted the offer. On the sixth night of his stay, Simpson was awakened by the smell of smoke. Nilsen lit a pair of jeans on fire in the kitchen and was calmly sitting down when Simpson got up to check on things. Nilsen told him that he must have dropped a lit cigarette.

In Nilsen's memoir, he described that moment as the time he was going to kill Simpson. He had planned to smother him with the smoldering jeans. Nilsen thought about the different ways he could kill Simpson: stab him with a kitchen knife, strangle him, or hit him over the head with a blunt object. But for some reason, he didn't try any of those methods. The next day, Simpson decided to leave Nilsen's apartment. He thought Nilsen was getting too weird.

The second man to escape the clutches of serial killer Dennis Nilsen was Japanese chef, Toshimitsu Ozawa. Nilsen thought that he met the chef at the Green Man Pub, which was located just a few blocks down from where Nilsen lived. The two connected, and went back to Nilsen's apartment for drinks and sex.

Ozawa later told police that the two of them were in Nilsen's flat drinking, when Nilsen calmly approached him holding a tie in his hands. Ozawa quickly stood up, kicked Nilsen in the groin, and ran out of the apartment. He went directly to the police to report the incident. The police questioned Nilsen but ended up closing the case as a lover's quarrel.

Stephen Sinclair

On January 26, 1983, Nilsen killed his final victim, 20-year-old Stephen Sinclair. It is unknown where or how they met, but witnesses claimed they saw the two men walking together into the Tube Station (London's rapid transit).

Nilsen claimed that Sinclair came over to his place to eat, drink, and watch a movie that was on television. They were watching the rock opera 'Tommy,' when Sinclair fell asleep in his armchair. Nilsen approached him and strangled the man with his necktie. After Sinclair died, and Nilsen was taking the clothing off the body, he noticed bandages wrapped around each of Sinclair's wrists. It looked as though Sinclair had tried to kill himself before.

Nilsen washed Sinclair's corpse in the bathtub, carried him to his bed, and sprinkled talcum powder all over him. He set up three mirrors around the bed so that no matter where he was lying, he could see both himself and Sinclair beside him. He watched until he fell asleep.

As with the previous victims, Nilsen dissected the body in the kitchen, placed different parts in plastic kitchen bags, and stored them in his closets and drawers throughout the house. He cooked some parts, such as the head, in a pot on the stove.

Nilsen disposed of the internal organs, flesh, and smaller bones by flushing them down the toilet, or in his bathtub drain.

On February 4, 1983, Nilsen wrote a complaint to the landlord stating that the drains at the apartment were constantly plugged and he required a plumber.

23 CRANLEY GARDEN APARTMENT

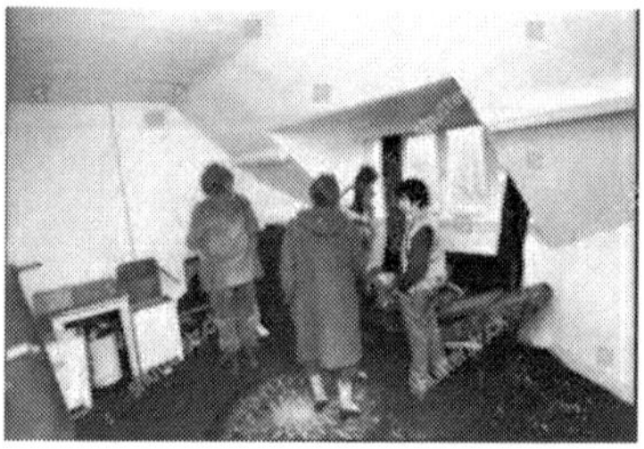

DENNIS NILSEN'S ATTIC APARTMENT

CHAPTER 4: THE INVESTIGATION

On the evening of Nilsen's arrest, police removed several large black plastic bags from his apartment. One of the bags contained two dissected torsos, and a smaller shopping bag full of internal organs. Another bag had a human skull with absolutely no flesh left on it. And yet another held a severed head and a torso with one arm still attached.

On February 10, Detective Peter Jay conducted an interview with Nilsen. During that interview, Nilsen admitted there were three corpses in his apartment: in his tea chest in the living room and in an upside-down drawer in his bathroom cabinet. A more thorough search found a lower torso with two legs in a duffle bag, hidden in the bathroom.

Nilsen couldn't identify who one of the men was, but the other two were 'John the Guardsman' and Stephen Sinclair. He admitted to Jay he started killing men in December of 1978, when he lived in his old apartment at 195 Melrose Avenue. When asked how many men he killed, he responded 12 or 13. And there were probably seven that he attempted to kill, but they managed to escape.

The detectives took Nilsen to his old residence at 195 Melrose Avenue so he could show them where he burned the remains of his victims. The police set up tents over the area and sent in a forensics unit to dig up the garden. They located over 1,000 fragments of human bones. Many were blackened from burning in the Nilsen's bonfires.

At 5:40 p.m., February 11, police formally charged Nilsen with the murder of Stephen Sinclair. His were the only prints they could identify within 48 hours. Under British law, police must charge their suspect within 48 hours of the arrest, or release them. The police made a statement to the press about Sinclair's murder; however, they did not mention how many other people they thought had been murdered by Nilsen.

Nilsen was given a legal aid lawyer to represent him, and the formal investigation began later that evening. Detectives interviewed Nilsen a total of 16 separate times, totaling just over 30 hours. Throughout the interviews, Nilsen claimed he had no idea why he had murdered the men. In fact, he was hoping that the police were going to be able to tell him why he had done it.

On almost every murder, his MO was the same. He had strangled the victim into unconsciousness, and then drowned them in his bathtub. He shaved off any hair that he found on the corpse, and applied make-up on the face to cover any blemish or scar that he noticed.

He then dressed the bodies in socks and underwear, and usually placed them laying face up on his bed. He sat on his victim's stomach and masturbated over the body. Nilsen said that with a few of the victims, he would also have intercrural sex (he would place his penis between the victim's thighs and thrust to create friction). He explained to the detectives that the bodies were too perfect to simply have common intercourse with them.

All the victim's personal items were destroyed after he would bathe the body. He did this as a cleansing ritual: a cleansing of their bodies, and of their identity. This made it easier to use them as a prop in his sexual fantasies. In regards to the conversations he had with the corpses, Nilsen admitted to often having full conversations while they were seated upright in an armchair. He told them the corpses about the kind of day he had, and all the interesting things he had done.

He described for detectives the disposal method he used while he lived at the Cranley Gardens apartment: he had to boil the heads in a large cooking pot in order to evaporate the internal contents, so that he didn't have to remove the brains and could keep them, the bodies would have to be dissected within a week usually and placed in plastic garbage bags, and finally the body organs and as much flesh as he could get off the bones would be flushed down the toilet.

At his old address on Melrose Avenue, however, he was able to keep the bodies for a much longer period of time before disposing of them. He would dissect them and place them in suitcases or plastic bags. He kept them outside in a shed that was located at the rear of his garden. There, he was also on the ground floor. So he was able to stow the bodies under the floorboards without anyone noticing them. Eventually, he burned them in a bonfire.

Nilsen also admitted that just before he dissected each of the bodies, he masturbated on them - a symbolic gesture of saying goodbye.

Before the interview ended, he was asked if he felt any remorse over all the killings. He said no. He firmly stated that he wished he was able to stop, but couldn't. He also said that it wasn't the act of killing that he took pleasure in, but it was the art of death that he worshipped.

Nilsen was remanded to Brixton Prison, located in the inner-South London area, and held there until his trial.

In an unusual statement, Nilsen claimed that under British law, he was innocent until proven guilty. Therefore, he would not wear a prison uniform. This was against prison rules. Nilsen protested by wearing no clothing at all. This led to the prison officials not being allowed to leave his cell since the prisoner was not wearing a prison uniform.

Other strange behavior ensued when on August 1, Nilsen threw his chamber pot out of his cell at the guards hitting several of them. He was arrested and charged with assaulting an officer, convicted on August 9, and sent to solitary confinement for 56 days.

By May 26, 1983, Nilsen was charged with five counts of murder and two attempted murders. Throughout the hearings leading up to the trial, he was represented by solicitor Ronald Moss, who he would fire and rehire several times. Nilsen had the idea that he could represent himself better than any lawyer could.

Ronald Moss wanted Nilsen to plead guilty on all charges. He initially agreed, but about five weeks before the trial, he decided to fire Moss again and pled not guilty. He hired a new attorney by the name of Ralph Haeems, who agreed that Nilsen was of diminished responsibility.

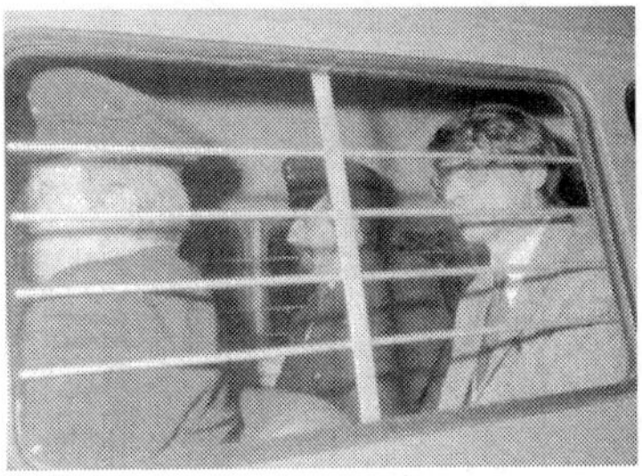

DENNIS NILSEN BEING TAKE TO TRIAL

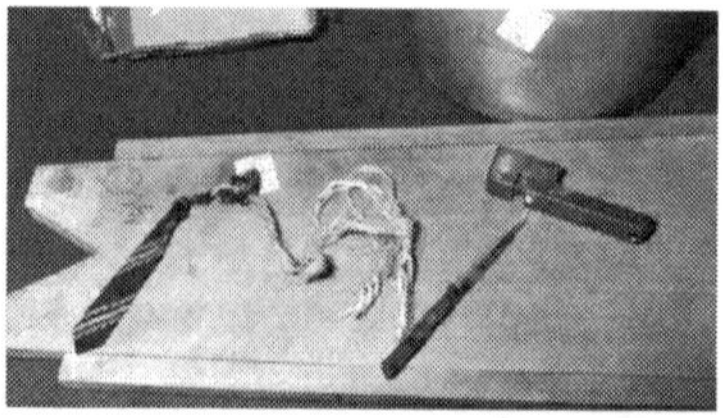

TRIAL EXHIBIT OF DAVID NILSEN'S KILLING TOOLS

TRIAL EVIDENCE PICTURE OF PLASTIC BAGS THAT WERE FULL OF BODY PARTS AT NILSEN'S APARTMENT

CHAPTER 5: TRIAL

On October 24, 1983, Dennis Nilsen was brought to trial at the Old Bailey Courthouse in London, presided over by Justice Croom-Johnson. He had six murder charges and two attempted murder charges against him. The trial began with the court administrator asking for Nilsen to give his plea to the crimes he was charged with. Nilsen answered, not guilty due to diminished responsibility.

Throughout the trial, the primary argument was not if Nilsen committed the murders or not, but what was his state of mind before, during and after the crimes. The prosecutor, Allen Green, argued that Nilsen was sane and in full control of his actions. He argued Nilsen killed with premeditation. The defense, now Ivan Lawrence, argued that Nilsen was incapable of forming the actual intention to commit murder, and should be convicted of manslaughter, not murder.

The prosecution's opening statement described the events in February 1983, when the plumbing company was called to the residence of 23 Cranley Gardens, and found human remains in the drainage system. The crown spoke of the subsequent arrest and confessions by Nilsen and the fact that after a thorough search of his premises, the remains of three more men were found. The crown also presented that on further questioning of Nilsen, he led them to 12 other victims killed at his old residence located at 195 Melrose Avenue. The key point in their argument was that Nilsen took so much time and effort to dispose of each of the bodies, that he could not have been incapable.

Green's opening statement for the defense used Nilsen's own statements he had made to the police during his interviews. The detective asked if he needed to kill and Nilsen responded that at the precise moment of the murder, he believed he was right in doing the act.

Douglas Stewart was the first witness to testify for the prosecution. He told the court that in November 1980, he had woken up in Nilsen's apartment, to find his ankles tied together, with Nilsen sitting on his stomach trying to strangle him with a tie. Stewart struggled and fought with Nilsen, and eventually was able to get control over him. According to Stewart, Nilsen screamed, "Take my money!" The prosecutor brought attention to this because it demonstrated that Nilsen was in the state of mind to think of a cover story in case his neighbors heard the noise. He could claim that Stewart was trying to rob him. Stewart escaped from the apartment, called the police, and reported the attack. The police questioned both Nilsen and Stewart but concluded that it was just a lover's quarrel between the two men.

The defense attempted to undermine Stewart's testimony by getting him to admit that he sold his story to some tabloid publications. They also argued because Stewart was so drunk that evening, he couldn't remember the details of what really happened.

The next day of the trial, the prosecution called two other men to the stand to testify about being attacked by Nilsen. The first of the men was Paul Nobbs. He told his story about going to Nilsen's apartment for drinks and sex. Nobbs told the jury that when he woke up, he had an awful headache, and noticed his face had bruises and was red. He testified that he didn't report the crime to the police since he was still 'in the closet' and didn't want it known that he was gay.

Carl Stottor was the second of the men to testify that day. Stottor testified that in May 1982, Nilsen attempted to strangle and then drown him. Stottor was extremely emotional during his examination by the court and needed several breaks to get through his story. He recounted how for two days, Nilsen choked him unconscious, and when he came to, Nilsen would do it again. He further told the jury how Nilsen held his head under the water in the bathtub, while he screamed out in fear, until he passed out.

Detective Chief Inspector Peter Jay took the

stand and recounted for the jury the circumstances surrounding Nilsen's arrest. He spoke of how calmly Nilsen confessed to the murders. Jay testified that it was very unusual for the accused to admit to such horrific crimes, let alone help to provide evidence. He went on to explain how Nilsen also took the police to where the bodies were left at his old residence.

Next up was Detective Superintendent Chambers, who read out Nilsen's formal confession to the court. This included the ritualistic and sexual acts he performed with his victims' bodies, the various ways he stored the bodies, and his methods of dismemberment and disposal. Several members of the jury were visibly upset over the descriptions given in this testimony, while Nilsen looked indifferent.

The trial resumed the next morning with the prosecution admitting several exhibits for the jury to see. They included the large pot that Nilsen would boil the heads in, and the cutting board from his kitchen used in the process of dismembering the bodies. The prosecution rested its case and turned the trial over to the defense.

The defense started with two psychiatrists on behalf of Nilsen. The first of these was Dr. James MacKeith who began his testimony with, "through a lack of emotional development, Nilsen experienced difficulty expressing any emotion other than anger, and his tendency to treat other human beings as components of his fantasies." He also explained how Nilsen associated unconscious bodies with sexual arousal, stating that Nilsen possessed narcissistic traits, an impaired sense of identity, and was able to depersonalize other people. In conclusion, MacKeith testified that Nilsen had an unidentified personality disorder severe enough to substantially reduce his responsibility.

The second psychiatrist to testify was Dr. Patrick Gallwey who diagnosed Nilsen with a 'borderline, false-self as if pseudo-normal, narcissistic personality disorder, with occasional outbreaks of schizoid disturbances that Nilsen managed most of the time to keep at bay. In conclusion, he argued that Nilsen was not guilty of malice aforethought. Under cross-examination, the focus was on what Nilsen's level of awareness was during the crimes. Dr. Gallwey claimed that Nilsen was aware of his actions, but due to his disorder, he did not appreciate the nature of his actions. The defense rested its' case on the science of psychiatry.

In rebuttal of the defense team's psychiatrist's testimonies, the prosecution called Dr. Paul Bowden to testify. Dr. Bowden had interviewed Nilsen on 16 separate occasions and for a total of 14 hours. Bowden testified that he found Nilsen to be abnormal in a colloquial sense, but said Nilsen was able to form relationships with people. He also testified that he found Nilsen was very manipulative.

Both the prosecution and defense gave their

closing arguments on November 3, 1983, and the jury retired to deliberate. The next day, they came back with a verdict of guilty on six counts of murder and two counts of attempted murder. Justice Croom-Johnson sentenced Nilsen to life imprisonment with a recommendation that he serve a minimum of 25 years.

CHAPTER 6: LIFE IN PRISON

Nilsen was transferred to the Wormwood Scrubs Prison, which is a category B men's prison located in the borough of Hammersmith, West London. He was considered a Category A prisoner, meaning he was given his own cell, but could mix freely with other inmates.

Nilsen did not appeal his conviction. He accepted the claims that he was able to control his own actions and that he had killed with premeditation. On the day he was convicted, he also admitted that he got an enormous thrill from all of it: the seduction, the luring of men back to his apartment, making the decision to kill, and even disposing of the body.

Nilsen was only in prison a month when in December 1983, he was attacked by another inmate. Albert Moffatt slashed Nilsen on his face and chest with a razor, a wound resulting in 89 stitches. He was transferred to Wakefield Prison, where he stayed until 1990. In 1993, he was transferred again to Whitemoor Prison. Nilsen was still a Category A prisoner, but now he was segregated from other prisoners.

In December 1994, the Home Secretary Michael Howard replaced Nilsen's sentence of life imprisonment with a minimum 25 years to Whole life. Again, Nilsen accepted this without appeal. In 2003, he was transferred to HMP Full Sutton where he remained incarcerated until his death on May 12, 2018.

After Nilsen died in prison, the prison authorities told the press that they had found over 200 letters in his cell. Those letters uncovered that he was having a sexual relationship with another inmate named 'Jimmy.'

CHAPTER 7: INTERVIEW WITH NILSEN

This is interview was taken by Central Television TV in 1993 in order to help British investigators understand the mind of the serial murderer. This is a great example of Nilsen's mindset about the murders.

INTERVIEWER: "How many young men did you kill?"

NILSEN: "When I was in the back of the police car going to the station after my arrest, they asked me how many there were. I didn't know so I give them a figure. Because I was cooperation with the police, I decided I'll stick with it. There were three of them invented so that the continuity of evidence to the police because I'm having to keep them happy."

INTERVIEWER: "So, what happened with the bodies of the men?"

NILSEN: " In the end, it was when I had two or three bodies under the floor boards, then come the summer it got hot and I knew there would be a smell problem, then I thought I'm going to have to deal with the smell problem. I thought what would cause the smell more than anything else, and I came to the conclusion that it was the innards. It was the soft parts of the body, you know the organs."

"So, on the weekend I would pull up the floorboards, and I'd find it totally unpleasant, so I would get blinding drunk, so I could face it and start the dissection on the kitchen floor. Then I'd have to go outside to be sick in the garden. "

INTERVIEWER: "What sort of preparation would you have to make for that? If you were to bring these young men into your kitchen and start to dismember them, that would leave an awful mess. "

NILSEN: "That doesn't leave a mess, why would it have to leave a mess?"

INTERVIEWER:" Well it could, couldn't it?"

NILSEN: "No, it doesn't leave amess, you see people in death situations where a knife is involved a lot of blood flying around. If I was to stab you right now, your heart is pumping away, so blood is splashing all over the place. In a dead body there's no blood spirts or anything like that, it congeals inside, and the 'flesh becomes like a butcher shop, there's little to no blood."

If you have a plastic bag you just must slip one of those under. You hold the body up and put the sheet under it, and then cut if up."

INTERVIEWER: So, if you take me now then to this first occasion when you have this young man, he's dead, you have bathed him.

NISLEN: He's now me, he's my body in the fantasies.

INTERVIEWER: So, now what do you do to him?

NILSEN: "Carry him in and make him appear even better, wrap him in cellophane to make him look better, it enhances the appearance in some way."

INTERVIEWER: "And then what?"

NILSEN: "Well I would undress him."

INTERVIEWER: "Well what would you do with the body? Would you leave it on the floor wrapped up, or would you do other things?"

NILSEN: "The most exciting part of the little conundrum was when I lifted the body, carried it. The expression of my power to life and carry and have control and the dangling elements of limp limbs was an expression of his facility. So, it was these two opposite things, I mean it was my power and his passivity, the more passive he would be, then the more powerful I was. "

"The bodies are all gone, there's nothing left, but I still feel that spiritual communion with these people."

Matthew Malekos wrote a thesis in March of 2012

called, "***The Birth of Psychopathy: Psychology of a Serial Killer – The Life of Dennis Nilsen.***" In his report, Malekos claimed that Nilsen showed great creativity in prison, therefore it indicated that his emotions were fully restored and functioning. He also believed the murders Nilsen committed, allowed him to see inside of him, which allowed the subsequent emotional development.

In one statement, the thesis claimed that the use of Nilsen's criminal activities and actions made him stronger and more optimistic than he was at the point of the murders. Malekos also argued that Nilsen had undergone a personal positive transformation while he has been incarcerated, not because of prison, but despite of prison.

In Russ Coffey's book "*Dennis Nilsen – Conversations with Britain's Most Evil Serial Killer,*" he brought attention to a very valid point ... though Nilsen might have showed some signs of character change while in prison, there remained many things very frightening about him. Such as on page 312 of Malekos' report, Nilsen wrote in a letter: "Yes, I am obsessed with remembering and enjoying the frisson of my sexual ritual, what else is there to do but caress my memories in my present social wasteland, I do not fantasize about other prisoners, but about the past."

CHAPTER 8: HISTORY OF A DROWNING BOY

In 2002, Nilsen asked his lawyer to send his manuscript to the Governor seeking approval to publish. Several months later, the book was confiscated and a letter was sent to Nilsen explaining why.

"The Prison Service has now read the manuscript and considered this request. It has decided not to allow the manuscript to be passed to Mr. Nilsen. The offenses are an integral part of the manuscript. The manuscript does not consist of serious representations about conviction or form part of serious comment about crime, the processes of justice or the penal system.

Rather it is a platform for Mr. Nilsen to denigrate people he dislikes. The withholding of the manuscript pursues a legitimate aim, namely the protection of morals, the protection of the reputation and rights of others, and the protection of information received in confidence."

Nilsen was angry over this decision and would later write to author Russ Coffey, "*I understand that many of the prison revelations in the book, including the interview with Central TV, will be embar-*

rassing to the Home Office. I care not about this. I do not play politics, I merely write testimony of a personal life. Although my body is imprisoned, they will not succeed in controlling the positive expression from my mind."

In 2003, Nilsen and his attorney decided to try a different approach and take the Prison Service to Judicial Review on the grounds that certain prison rules violated his basic freedom of expression. Was this a real concern for Nilsen? Did he really care about being able to express his thoughts to the world, or was it about gaining more attention to himself? During his arrest and trial there was a media deluge around him that he had never experienced before, and he loved the attention. He interviewed and wrote to anybody that would talk to him or accept his letters.

Nilsen's and his lawyer's plan was to challenge clause '5b' of the prison rules, which prohibits prisoners' from sending out any material for publishing if it is about their own crime or past offences. The only exception would be when the correspondence consisted of 'serious representations about a conviction or sentence.'

Russ Coffey wrote to Nilsen and gained access to his manuscript through a man named Johnny Marling. He also gave Coffey access to a series of essays, letters, pictures, and tapes by Nilsen. He was hired by the Sunday Times magazine to do a 5,000-word feature article for them.

Marling connected with Nilsen after reading the book *"Killing for Company"* by Brian Masters. He contacted Nilsen through letters to the prison. The two of them hit it off right away, since Marling lived in Cricklewood, and they built their relationship from there. Marling visited Nilsen in prison whenever he was able to.

In October 2003, Judge Maurice Kay heard the case and took only two days to rule that the Human Rights Act had not been infringed on, and he could see no reason for the manuscript to be returned to Nilsen.

His manuscript on life as a prisoner was at about 4,500 pages at last count before his death.

Epilogue

On May 12, 2018, serial killer Dennis Nilsen, also known as the 'Muswell Hill Murderer' or 'Kindly Killer' died in prison at the age of 72. He was 34 years into his life sentence at HMP Full Sutton Prison. According to authorities, he died from natural causes.

The house at 23 Cranley Gardens has been on the market and sold many times since the murders. Quite often, the residents of the house complain about strange noises and weird movements throughout the house. They end up selling within a year. The house never sells for the value it should in that area. Nobody wants to live where so many men were killed, dissected and disposed of. It usually lists for around £300,000, but the other houses in the area sell for £800,000 or more. At the time of writing this book, it is lived in. But the top floor attic room that Nilsen lived in is still empty. There is always flowers in the window.

Shortly after Nilsen's death, George Bamby-Salvador claimed to have the final letter written by serial killer Nilsen. Salvador put the letter on display at the Crime Museum in London, otherwise known as the 'Black Museum,' which is in the New

Scotland Yard headquarters.

Salvador entered into letter correspondence with Nilsen after Nilsen discovered that Salvador was the son of Charles Bronson Salvador – the most violent prisoner in Britain. Bronson was originally incarcerated for armed bank robbery. Since then, he has attacked so many prison guards, he has been sentenced to life imprisonment.

Salvador claims that it was after he made a television appearance in January 2017, claiming to be the son of Charles Bronson Salvador, that Nilsen contacted him. The two men exchanged eight letters in total before Nilsen died. The final letter was dated February 2018.

Nilsen wrote about his links to West Country, an area of South Western England, because of his time in the army on Dartmoor. The letter also had a large verse poem that was mainly reminiscent of his life there, including seagulls, the decline in the fishing industry, and even Brexit:

"As a boy soldier in the early 1960's I spent three summer camps at Fort Tregantal in Cornwall and also completed exercises in Dartmoor, where I often route-marched past the prison, but didn't go in later, in 1968-69 I was posted, with the Argyll and Sutherland Highlanders, to Plymouth at Seaton Barracks in Crownhill, after I returned from Aden in South Yemen where a rebellion had just ended with its independence. "I grew fond of the ambiance of the West Coun-

try character in all my 11 years in the army. "

The letter continued with ramblings about the seagulls hitting tourists with poop droppings, and how the people who live in the city should hold onto their 'pasties' (patches that cover the nipples). Nilsen warned the people of England they better leave the European Union before it was too late.

The note was signed as 'Den Nilsen' and appears to be his real signature. Salvador claims the letter is 100% genuine, and is extremely rare because Nilsen was not known for sharing his thoughts freely with many people. Salvador now has all the letters from Nilsen displayed at his own real crime museum in Torque.

Salvador made the statement:

"At the end of the day he was a murderer, necrophile and complete lunatic and there is no hiding from that, but with my interest in crime, to be able to communicate directly with probably the most infamous serial killer was a fascinating experience.

When he sent a letter, I replied because I just wanted to find out a little bit more about him. He mentions his link to Plymouth, and I wanted to know who his friend was in Pakington (another town in South West Country)."

Salvador claims *"Nilsen reveals more about his crimes in other letters. He tried to portray to me that what he did was just that, something he did, and he didn't mean anything by it. It was peculiar, and he was almost blasé about it. It was like me or you just explaining about going out to the cinema or down to the pub."*

Salvador also says the letter gave little indication that Nilsen was dying, though he did mention a stomach complaint and not being able to write for a while but nothing to indicate that it was terminal.

Other Books by Alan

Beyond Suspicion: Russell Williams: A Canadian Serial Killer

#1 Bestselling Book in True Crime Depositions

Young girl's panties started to go missing; sexual assaults began to occur, and then female bodies were found! Soon this quiet town of Tweed, Ontario, was in panic. What's even more shocking was when an upstanding resident stood accused of the assaults. This was not just any man, but a pillar of the community; a decorated military pilot who had flown Canadian Forces VIP aircraft for dignitaries such as the Queen of England, Prince Philip, the Governor General and the Prime Minister of Canada.

This is the story of serial killer Russell Williams, the elite pilot of Canada's Air Force One, and the innocent victims he murdered. Unlike other serial killers, Williams seemed very unaffected about his crimes and leading two different lives.

Alan R. Warren describes the secret life including the abductions, rape and murders that were unleashed on an unsuspecting community. Included are letters written to the victims by Williams and descriptions of the assaults and rapes as seen on videos and photos taken by Williams during the attacks.

This updated version also contains the full brilliant police interrogation of Williams and his confession. Also, the twisted way in which Williams planned to pin his crimes on his unsuspecting neighbor.

Amazon United States
Amazon Canada
Amazon United Kingdom

Deadly Betrayal: The True Story of Jennifer Pan - Daughter from Hell

Find out what really happened when seasoned true crime reporter and author, Alan R. Warren, takes you through the details as they unfold in this book of a Deadly Betrayal.

A family of three tied up, each with a gun to their head. "Where's the money? Where's the fucking money?" one of the intruders yelled. A petrified daughter tortured and forced to listen to her parents being shot in cold blood. "I heard shots, like pops," she told the 911 operator, "somebody's broke into our home, please, I need help!" Was this a home invasion? Or something else, more sinister, a Deadly Betrayal.

The real-life horror story that happened inside the Pan family home shocked their normally peaceful upscale Toronto neighborhood. The Pans were an example of an immigrant family. Hann and his wife, Bich Pan, fled from Vietnam to Canada after the U.S.-Vietnamese war to find a better life. Their daughter, Jennifer, was an Olympic-caliber figure skater, an award-winning pianist, and a straight A student.

The Pans worked their way up in this ragsto-riches story, now living in a beautiful home with luxury cars in the driveway. Was it these expensive items that lured three intruders with guns into their home on the night of November 8, 2010?

Amazon United States
Amazon Canada
Amazon United Kingdom

View ALL BOOKS by the Author at:

https://www.amazon.com/Alan-R.-Warren/e/B01LG8S48Y

Grindr Serial Killer: Stephen Port (British Criminals)

In today's world where meeting people for the purpose of having sex with a simple click on your phone, a new type of gay sex called 'Party N Play' or 'Chemsex' has become all the rage in the mainstream.

Several young gay men were being found dead, appearing to have overdosed on the favorite sex drugs used at these chemsex parties, in a city church yard in east London. Was this what the metro police claimed it was, "a sex drug overdose," or was there something more going on here?

It would soon be discovered that a popular 41-year-old, Stephen Port, who had appeared on 'Celebrity Chef UK' would be arrested and charged with four of the young men's murders by overdosing them with GBH, 'The Date Rape Drug,' enough to kill the men, and then raping them and leaving their bodies out in a church yard.

Since the conviction of Celebrity Chef UK, Stephen Port, the police are now reviewing 58 other mysterious deaths by overdose where the body was found dead in the same area of London. There are now 17 police officers under investigation for not investigating the crimes because of their homophobia.

Included are several of the personal letters convicted serial killer Stephen Port sent to his friend and pen pal Cody Lachey which reveals what he claims happened to each of the victims and what really happened in these Chemsex parties. You will also find out some of Port's personal details that you wouldn't expect to hear.

Amazon United States
Amazon Canada
Amazon United Kingdom

About the Author

Alan R. Warren has written several Best-Selling True Crime books and has been one of the hosts and producer of the popular NBC news talk radio show 'House of Mystery' which reviews True Crime, History, Science, Religion, Paranormal Mysteries that we live with every day from a darker, comedic and logical perspective and has interviewed guests such as Robert Kennedy Jr., F. Lee Bailey, Aphrodite Jones, Marcia Clark, Nancy Grace, Dan Abrams and Jesse Ventura. The show is based in Seattle on KKNW 1150 A.M. and syndicated on the NBC network throughout the United States including on KCAA 106.5 F.M. Los Angeles/Riverside/Palm Springs, as well in Utah, New Mexico, and Arizona.

References

1.Nicholson, David (5 November 1983). "Nilsen given 25-year sentence". *The Times* (61682). London.

2.https://en.wikipedia.org/wiki/The_Press_and_Journal_(Scotland)

3.Edison, N.J. (2003). *The World's Most Infamous Killers*. London, England: Chancellor ISBN 978-0-753-70715-9.

4.*Dennis Nilsen: Conversations With Britain's Most Evil Serial Killer* ISBN 978-1-782-19459-0

5.Tweedie, Neil (10 November 2006). "Nilsen describes how he murdered his first victim". *The Daily Telegraph*. London.

6.Marriott, Trevor (2012). *The Evil Within*. London: Blake. ISBN 978-1-857-82798-9.

7.Coffey, Russ (5 August 2013). *Dennis Nilsen – Conversations with Britain's Most Evil Serial Killer*. John Blake Publishing. ISBN 9781782197195.

8.Davidson, Lauren (12 November 2015). "Would you buy the former flat of one of Britain's worst serial killers?" – via www.telegraph.co.uk.

9.Professor David Bowen". *The Sunday Telegraph*. London. 12 April 2011.

10.Dennis Nilsen's First Kill". channel5.com. 23 December 2015.

11.Born to Kill: Series 3 – Episode 5". *radiotimes.com*. 10 June 2012.

12. "Serial Killers: Dennis Nilsen (2009) – Crime Documentary".

13. "TV Show Time: Real Crime". *tvtime.com*. 21 December 2003.

14. The Black Museum (1988)". bfi.co.uk. 9 October 2009.

15. Ramsland, Katherine. "A Taste for Death". *truTV*.

16. Nigel, Cawthorne; Cawthorne, Nigel (7 August 2014). *Bodies in the Back Garden – True Stories of Brutal Murders Close to Home*. John Blake Publishing. ISBN 9781784181796.

17. "Serial killer Dennis Nilsen's last moments heard as inquest opens". *Hull Daily Mail*. 18 May 2018

18. ^ Higgens, Dave (19 May 2018). "Serial Killer Dennis Nilsen Died in Hospital After an Operation". *The Times*.

19. "Nilsen v Full Sutton Prison & Anor [2004] EWCA Civ 1540". *BAILII*. 17 November 2004.

20. Dennis Nilsen: Serial killer dies in prison aged 72". *BBC News*. 12 May 2018.

21. Nicholson, David (5 November 1983). "The lonely murderer who preyed on young drifters". *The Times* (61682). London.

22. Grim Search for London Murder Victims". *The New York Times*. 11 February 1983.

35012984R00052

Made in the USA
Lexington, KY
30 March 2019